GALE
CENGAGE Learning

Novels for Students, Volume 43

Project Editor: Sara Constantakis Rights Acquisition and Management: Robyn Young Composition: Evi Abou-El-Seoud Manufacturing: Rhonda Dover

Imaging: John Watkins

Product Design: Pamela A. E. Galbreath, Jennifer Wahi Digital Content Production: Allie Semperger Product Manager: Meggin Condino © 2013 Gale, Cengage Learning

For product information and technology assistance, contact us at **Gale Customer Support, 1-800-877-4253.**

For permission to use material from this text or product, submit all requests online at www.cengage.com/permissions.

Further permissions questions can be e-mailed to **permissionrequest@cengage.com** While every effort has been made to ensure the reliability of the information presented in this publication, Gale, a part of Cengage Learning, does not guarantee the accuracy of the data contained herein. Gale accepts no payment for listing; and inclusion in the publication of any organization, agency, institution, publication, service, or individual does not imply endorsement of the editors or publisher. Errors brought to the attention of the publisher and verified to the satisfaction of the publisher will be corrected in future editions.

Gale
27500 Drake Rd.
Farmington Hills, MI, 48331-3535

ISBN-13: 978-1-4144-9486-9
ISBN-10: 1-4144-9486-6
ISSN 1094-3552

This title is also available as an e-book.

ISBN-13: 978-1-4144-9272-8
ISBN-10: 1-4144-9272-3
Contact your Gale, a part of Cengage Learning sales
representative for ordering information.

Printed in Mexico
1 2 3 4 5 6 7 17 16 15 14 13

The Samurai's Garden

Gail Tsukiyama 1995

Introduction

The Samurai's Garden (1995), by Gail Tsukiyama, tells the story of Stephen Chan, a Chinese college student recovering from tuberculosis. The novel consists of Stephen's journal entries starting in September of 1937, when he arrives at his family's vacation house in a small seaside town in Japan, and continuing into autumn of the following year, when he leaves, having healed physically and matured emotionally.

While Stephen is there, he is befriended by Matsu, who has been caretaker of the house and garden since he was a young man. Stephen also has his first brush with romance, all the while worrying about the Japanese soldiers fighting their way through China toward his family in Hong Kong. As Stephen learns to find his place in the world, Tsukiyama explores themes of personal and cultural identity, isolation, and family over the threatening background of the war. *The Samurai's Garden* also reflects Tsukiyama's own heritage as an Asian American with both Chinese and Japanese cultural influences.

Author Biography

Tsukiyama was born in San Francisco on September 13, 1957. Her father was a Japanese American who was raised in Hawaii, and her mother was of Chinese descent, having immigrated to the United States from Hong Kong. Thus Tsukiyama's life was rich with both of her parents' cultural backgrounds, and it clearly had a great influence on her work.

Tsukiyama began writing as a teenager. She mostly created poetry, but when she started college at San Francisco State University, she first studied film. After deciding that writing allowed her to express herself creatively better than film, she changed her major to creative writing. She earned her bachelor's degree and then continued on at San Francisco State to earn her master's. Her master's thesis was a collection of poetry, but soon after finishing school, Tsukiyama switched to prose. She began to write short stories and soon started work on a novel.

Her first published book, *Women of the Silk* (1991), became a best seller. *The Samurai's Garden* (1994) was her second book; her most recent work is *A Hundred Flowers* (2012). Many of Tsukiyama's novels take place in the past or in very specific communities. For example, *Women of the Silk* and its sequel, *The Language of Threads* (1999), recount the lives of Chinese silk workers in the first half of the twentieth century. The characters in *The Street of a Thousand Blossoms* (2007) provide glimpses into the Japanese traditions of sumo wrestling and Noh theater. *In The Samurai's Garden*, which takes place in the late 1930s, readers see the citizens of Yamaguchi, all of whom have been afflicted with leprosy. To add to the realism of her stories and their historical settings, Tsukiyama researches her topics extensively.

In addition to being a fiction author, Tsukiyama has taught creative writing at her alma mater, San Francisco State University. She also writes book reviews and has worked as a judge and then the chairperson for the Kiriyama Pacific Rim book award panel. In addition to popular success, she has received several critical awards, including the Academy of American Poets Award and the PEN Oakland/Josephine Miles Literary Award.

Tsukiyama still lives and works in her home state of California. As quoted in *A to Z of American Women Writers*, by Carol Kort, Tsukiyama calls herself "as American as apple pie." However, like many Americans, she is a mix of cultures: "All the Chinese traditions from my mother's side of the family are within me, and have somehow found expression through my books."

Plot Summary

The novel is told in the form of Stephen's diary. The first entry is dated September 15, 1937, and the setting is indicated: Tarumi, Japan. The book is also divided into sections by seasons of the year.

Autumn

The reader meets the narrator Stephen Chan, who has just arrived at his family's vacation home in Japan. He describes how he became ill at school in Canton, went home to Hong Kong, and now has been sent to recover in the cooler, drier climate of the seaside town of Tarumi. Stephen is still suffering from some of the effects of tuberculosis: coughing, fevers, and weakness, and his parents are worried about him. There is a brief mention of Stephen's brother and sisters: Anne, Henry, and Penelope, who is nicknamed Pie. The children were given Christian names because Stephen's "father believes it an asset in the business world to be addressed with ease by Westerners."

Stephen describes his journey. He stopped briefly in Kobe to see his father, who spends much of his time in Japan on business, and then continued by train to Tarumi, where he was met by Matsu, the "caretaker of the beach house." Matsu is quiet but polite, and he tries to make Stephen feel at home. His work includes everything from tending the garden, which he loves, to cooking and drawing Stephen's baths. The next day Stephen finds his way around, describing the house in his journal and walking to the beach. While he is there, he sees two girls running and laughing on the sand. Stephen's father comes to visit after a few days, and they discuss Japan's attacks on China. Stephen is curious about Matsu because he does not talk about himself, but Mr. Chan does not know much about him.

Stephen is sad when his father leaves, so Matsu invites him to come on a visit to a friend in another village, Yamaguchi. Stephen is concerned when he learns that it is a "Village of Lepers," but Matsu assures him that leprosy cannot be spread by casual contact. The houses in the village are shabby and "mismatched." Stephen sees the sores and bandages of the people who live there and tries not to be afraid or stare rudely.

Matsu introduces Stephen to Sachi, who lives in a nice house set a little bit outside the rest of the village. Stephen sees that Sachi is beautiful in spite of the places where her skin is damaged by leprosy. On the walk home, Matsu explains that he lost his younger sister to the disease and that he has taken care of Sachi ever since she moved to Yamaguchi.

Matsu works in his garden while Stephen paints and goes to the beach. He meets Keiko and Mika, the sisters he saw there earlier. Another visit to Yamaguchi cements Stephen's fascination with Sachi, and Matsu tells Stephen a little more of her story: she left her family when she contracted leprosy and never saw them again. Matsu introduces

Stephen to his friend Kenzo, who runs the tea house in Tarumi. He was also friends with Sachi, but she would not see him once she got sick.

Stephen receives a letter from his mother in which she tells him of her suspicion that his father has been having an affair. Stephen is very upset and does not completely believe her. A storm hits Tarumi, and Stephen is injured while trying to help Matsu prepare the house to withstand the bad weather. Concerned for Stephen, Sachi ventures out of Yamaguchi for the first time since she moved there to visit him. The storm has ruined Matsu's garden, and Sachi and Stephen both work to help him repair the damage.

Stephen sees Keiko again, and they plan to meet in secret on the beach. They take a walk together, and Keiko tells him that her brother is with the Japanese army in China. It makes them both quiet. Keiko will not let Stephen walk her home because she does not want her parents to know she has met him.

When Stephen returns to the beach house, Kenzo is there. He has seen Sachi and is very angry. He shoves Matsu and calls Sachi a "monster" when he sees her face without the scarf she usually wears. Matsu throws Kenzo out of the garden, and Sachi goes home to Yamaguchi. Matsu explains to Stephen that Kenzo and Sachi were once engaged. When she became ill, Kenzo "didn't have the courage to face" her, so Matsu became their go-between. Kenzo was angry because Matsu had led him to believe Sachi would never leave Yamaguchi and then Kenzo found her visiting Matsu.

Media Adaptations

- *The Samurai's Garden* was produced in 2004 as an audiobook on CD from Recording for the Blind and Dyslexic.

Winter

Stephen visits Sachi on his own. He tries to convince Sachi that she has done nothing wrong by visiting Matsu, but she insists that she has dishonored herself, Stephen, and Matsu. Stephen touches the scars on her face in an effort to convince her that they make no difference to him. Sachi shows Stephen her garden, which Matsu helped her create. It is a rock garden rather than one of plants and trees. She encourages him to try raking patterns into the pebbles, and it does indeed help soothe him.

Sachi tells him about the death of Tomoko, Matsu's sister. She was one of the first to show the symptoms of leprosy, and she committed *seppuku*, a traditional suicide ritual, because she could not live with the feeling that she had shamed her family. Sachi and Tomoko had been good friends, but Sachi largely ignored Matsu until after his sister died. Knowing how close the girls were, Matsu brought Tomoko's "lucky stone," which matches one that Sachi has. Sachi explains how she and Tomoko "found them when we were young girls and always associated them with good luck and all the other dreams of youth."

When Stephen returns home, Matsu tells him that his father has arrived for a visit. Stephen is nervous, not wanting to confront him with his mother's accusations that he is having an affair. Mr. Chan compliments Stephen's painting, which surprises and embarrasses Stephen, because his father usually thinks little of Stephen's art. Mr. Chan brings up the issue of the affair, admits that there is another woman, and says that Stephen's mother "was never to have known." Mr. Chan says that nothing will change, that he will continue to spend time both with his family in Hong Kong and with his mistress, Yoshiko, in Kobe. In the evening, they discuss the war, but before Stephen wakes in the morning, his father has left.

Matsu and Stephen visit the Shinto shrine in another village. Matsu prays and encourages

Stephen to do so as well. On the walk home, Stephen discovers that Matsu knew about his father's mistress and becomes angry. The Christmas and New Year's holidays pass quietly, and Stephen receives a letter from his friend King. It is full of news about the fighting in China and a terrible massacre in Nanking, and Stephen is shocked by it —he has heard only the Japanese news broadcasts, which did not mention the massacre.

Stephen and Matsu attend a village celebration of the beginning of spring, but the festivities are interrupted by the news that Kenzo has killed himself. Matsu, even through his shock and grief, cares for Stephen, who felt ill after hearing of Kenzo's death. Matsu tells Stephen that he went to Yamaguchi to bring the terrible news to Sachi. She was saddened but will not come to the funeral. Matsu finds some comfort in his garden. The entire village attends Kenzo's funeral. Stephen sees Keiko there but does speak with her because she is with her parents. Stephen spies Sachi—she comes to pay her respects to Kenzo after all, but no one else sees her. Keiko comes to visit Stephen briefly later and promises to see him again soon.

Spring

Stephen and Matsu go to visit Sachi and find Yamaguchi in the middle of a crisis, a fire. Stephen helps one of the village men, Hiro, to carry buckets of water, and the fire is put out, but not before several houses are destroyed. Matsu and Stephen spend the night at Hiro's house. Stephen goes to see Sachi and promises her that he will never tell Matsu that she attended Kenzo's funeral. Sachi tells him the story of her life: when she first met Matsu, how her friendship grew with his sister Tomoko, how she began to fall in love with Kenzo, and what happened when she noticed the first signs of leprosy.

Sachi kept the disease a secret from everyone except Matsu, who tried to help her as much as he could. When Sachi finally decided to tell Kenzo, it was too much for him. She tried to commit suicide with some other people from the village who were also afflicted. Many held the belief that those with leprosy were somehow shaming their families. Sachi and four others walked into the sea; the others drowned, but she could not do it. "The greatest honor I could have given my family was that of my death, and I ran from it," she tells Stephen.

Sachi ran away and hid in the woods. Matsu found her and took her to Yamaguchi. At first Sachi was frightened and disgusted by the wounds of the villagers, but she lived with Michiko, a patient and kind elder, who took care of Sachi but was also honest with her, telling her, "There aren't many choices for us." Sachi, with the help of Michiko and Matsu, learned to rebuild her life. After Michiko died, Matsu helped Sachi build her rock garden.

Matsu and Stephen provide supplies and help the villagers of Yamaguchi rebuild after the fire. Stephen receives a letter from his mother explaining that she and Pie will not visit for the summer as planned because Mr. and Mrs. Chan are "still sorting everything out." When the homes in Yamaguchi are rebuilt, there is a big celebration that Stephen calls "one of the best nights of my life."

Summer

The weather gets warmer. Stephen and Matsu walk into Tarumi, and Stephen sees Keiko. They make plans to meet at the Shinto shrine. When Stephen and Matsu return home, Sachi is there to tell them that Hiro has died. Matsu insists that Stephen does not need to attend the funeral. Matsu has still not returned from Yamaguchi when Stephen has to leave to meet Keiko. Keiko brings refreshments. She and Stephen have a romantic picnic.

Stephen's father visits. They make small talk until Stephen asks about the war. He is concerned about his mother and sister alone in Hong Kong. Mr. Chan says that he and Mrs. Chan have agreed that Stephen should stay at the beach house through the summer. He believes there is no danger of the fighting reaching their home.

Stephen plans to take part in Tarumi's Obon festival, during which people return to their hometown to visit the graves of their ancestors and have a big celebration. Matsu's sister Fumiko comes for the festival. Fumiko is much more talkative than her brother. She insists on preparing lunch when she arrives and talks to Stephen about Matsu as she cooks.

Early the next morning, they go to the cemetery, where the townspeople clean their families' grave sites and leave tea, sake, and food. Then everyone returns to the village, which is decorated with paper lanterns. There is laughter and dancing and food, but Stephen seems melancholy. He sees Kenzo's dark tea house and thinks of the people in Yamaguchi and the people being killed in the war in China.

Autumn

The weather begins to turn, and the summer visitors begin to leave Tarumi. Stephen meets Keiko on the beach, and she tells him that they cannot be together. Her brother was killed while fighting in China, and she knows that her family would not accept her falling in love with a Chinese boy.

Stephen and Matsu go to Yamaguchi to visit Sachi. Stephen watches Matsu check Sachi's home for problems, like the heavy fall rain leaking through the roof, and realizes that Matsu is "the master of the house" even though he would say he does not even live there.

Stephen receives a letter from King, who describes the fighting as "awfully hot." He tells Stephen that some items are being rationed because of shortages caused by the war and that a girl they knew in school was killed. The letter disturbs Stephen—he cannot remember the girl from school, but hearing details of life at home brings the war to life for him. There is also a letter from his father, who invites Stephen on a business trip to Tokyo.

Tokyo seems huge to Stephen after over a year in Tarumi and Yamaguchi. Stephen walks around the city streets, sees the Imperial Palace, and feels he has to keep his voice down when speaking to his father in Chinese. Mr. Chan suggests that Stephen should probably return to Hong Kong before Christmas. While they are at their hotel, Stephen and his father hear on the radio that the Chinese city of Canton has fallen to the Japanese army. After such news, they feel they had better leave Tokyo.

Knowing that he will soon be going home, Stephen goes to Yamaguchi to say goodbye to Sachi. They go to the garden, and Stephen moves the pebbles with a rake. He asks Sachi, "Who will take care of you if something happens to Matsu?" She reassures him. Sachi tells Stephen that he has given her and Matsu something very important: he has become like their child, the one they "lost so many years ago." Stephen feels sadness for his friends for the grief they must have felt for their stillborn child.

Stephen gives Sachi a beautiful vase as a gift. In return, she gives him the two lucky stones that she and Tomoko had found when they were young. Stephen spends one last day on the beach. He cannot imagine how it will be when he returns to Hong Kong. Sachi comes down to the beach house for one last goodbye, which makes Stephen very happy.

On Stephen's last afternoon in Tarumi, he and

Matsu go to the Shinto shrine in Tama and have dinner together. The next morning, Stephen takes a few minutes to appreciate Matsu's garden, remembering the comfort it brought him when he first arrived at the house. Stephen finds a white flower on the garden gate and knows that it is Keiko's way of saying goodbye.

Matsu walks Stephen to the train station. It is difficult for them to say goodbye. Once the train pulls away, Stephen finds a gift Matsu has tucked in among his other belongings, two leather-bound journals. As the train carries him on the first leg of his journey home, Stephen begins writing, starting the new chapter of his life as his time in Tarumi comes to an end.

Characters

Anne Chan

Anne is Stephen's older sister. She does not appear in the story directly, but Stephen thinks of her at her school in Macao.

Henry Chan

Henry is Stephen's younger brother. Like Anne, he is at school in Macao and does not appear in the story.

Mr. Chan

Mr. Chan is Stephen's father. He travels back and forth between the family home in Hong Kong and Kobe, Japan, for his work. Stephen sometimes thinks his father seems "more Japanese than Chinese." Mr. Chan is a businessman and very practical. He does not seem interested in things he finds frivolous, such as Stephen's painting, which he considers a "time-consuming hobby." Stephen and his father seem to have a difficult time talking to one another. Their relationship is made more strained when Stephen learns that his father has kept a mistress in Kobe for twelve years. Mr. Chan insists that nothing about their lives will change, even though Stephen and his mother know about the affair, but it changes the way Stephen views his father.

Mrs. Chan

Mrs. Chan is Stephen's mother. She is a nervous woman who does not seem close to her children. When Stephen thinks of family vacations at the beach house when he was young, he remembers his mother on her own in the garden, suffering from the heat. When Mrs. Chan suspects her husband of having an affair, she writes Stephen and asks him to confront Mr. Chan. In fact, her letters seem to be full of her own complaints and worries rather than interest in and concern for her son.

Penelope Chan

Penelope, known as Pie, is Stephen's little sister. She is a bright, cheerful girl, and Stephen is close to her. Part of the reason Stephen is sent away to recover from tuberculosis is to protect Pie from contagion, because she cannot resist coming into his room to talk to him. She writes him a letter telling him that she is doing work for the Red Cross because of the war in China. When Stephen is preparing to leave Tarumi, he tries to find a gift to bring home to her.

Stephen Chan

Stephen is the narrator of the story. Most of the

book is Stephen's diary, so it is from his point of view. He is a young man who has been ill with tuberculosis, an infection of the lungs that causes fevers and persistent coughing. Stephen's family sends him to their vacation home in Japan to recover. While Stephen is there, he swims in the ocean, sketches and paints, and falls in love for the first time.

The most significant relationship in the book is Stephen's friendship with Matsu, the caretaker of the beach house. Stephen learns a lot from Matsu and through him is introduced to Sachi and all of the villagers who live in Yamaguchi. Meeting the people whose lives have been changed by leprosy and especially having Matsu as an example highlight for Stephen the important things in life: inner strength, loyalty, and kindness rather than physical appearance or social position.

The novel is the story of Stephen's coming of age. Although he becomes disillusioned with his father, who has been secretly keeping a mistress for twelve years, Stephen tries to handle the situation in a mature manner. From his first romance, he learns about love, and when the young woman breaks up with him, he learns a little about heartbreak. In the year that Stephen spends in Japan, he becomes an adult.

Ching

Ching is the Chan family's servant. Although she is an employee, she has been with the Chans so long she is like a member of the family. Stephen explains that "my mother told Ching secrets, then listened to her like a wise older sister."

Fumiko

Fumiko is Matsu's sister. She comes to Yamaguchi near the end of the novel for the Obon festival. She is more talkative than her brother, and it makes Stephen happy to see Matsu with someone who knows him so well and loves him.

Keiko Hagashi

Keiko is the older of the two sisters that Stephen meets on the beach. She is beautiful and shy, but she likes Stephen and agrees to meet him on several occasions. She keeps her meetings with Stephen secret from her parents. Near the end of the novel, Keiko tells Stephen she cannot see him anymore, but before he departs from Tarumi, she leaves a flower for him on the garden gate to say goodbye. Through his romance with Keiko, Stephen learns about both love and loss.

Mika Hagashi

Mika is Keiko's younger sister. When Stephen first sees them on the beach, they seem to enjoy each other's company, but later, when Keiko wants to meet Stephen alone, she thinks of Mika as a nosy pest. Keiko tricks Mika so that she can go out without her.

Toshiro Hagashi

Toshiro is Keiko and Mika's brother. Stephen learns fairly early on in his relationship with Keiko that Toshiro is fighting with the Japanese army in China. He does not appear in the story, but he is significant because his death in the war makes Keiko conclude that she and Stephen cannot be together.

Hiro

Hiro is one of the villagers in Yamaguchi Although he has lost one of his hands to leprosy, he is strong, and Stephen is impressed when he helps Hiro while fighting the fire. When Hiro dies, Matsu thinks Stephen would be too tired to come to the funeral. Sachi tells Stephen not to think of Hiro's death but to remember his life: "Hold on to your last memory of Hiro-*san*, the night of the celebration when he was happiest and most alive."

Kenzo

Kenzo has known Matsu and Sachi since they were very young. He owns the teahouse in Tarumi. Kenzo and Sachi were engaged to be married when she contracted leprosy. Kenzo could not face her disease, and Matsu took over as her caretaker and protector, but Kenzo stayed loyal to her in his own way, never marrying. Matsu always led Kenzo to believe that Sachi would never leave Yamaguchi, but Kenzo comes to the beach house and sees Sachi in the garden there. He is angry and pushes Matsu, feeling betrayed and likely feeling ashamed of his own disgust at Sachi's disfigurement. He calls her a "monster." After the confrontation in the garden, Kenzo will not speak to Matsu. He hangs himself in the teahouse because of his anger and confusion.

King

King is Stephen's friend from college. Unlike Stephen's father, King seems to understand why painting is important to Stephen. King does not appear in the story, but he sends Stephen letters that make him miss his old life. The letters also tell Stephen what is going on with the war in China, giving a personal perspective to the announcements Stephen hears on Matsu's radio.

Matsu

After Stephen, Matsu is the most important character in the novel. He is a quiet man, and when Stephen first meets him, he thinks that Matsu "seems the type of man who's more comfortable alone, and it's not hard to figure out that he must be annoyed at my disturbing his tranquil world." However, Matsu's reserved exterior hides a huge heart. Sachi says, "With Matsu, everything is in what he does not say." In Matsu's actions, we can see the sort of person he is.

Matsu spends his life helping other people and tending the plants in his garden. When he was a very young man, he fell in love with Sachi, but he stood aside when she chose Kenzo. When Sachi realized that she had leprosy, it was Matsu who helped her, speaking with the doctor and then taking her to Yamaguchi and helping her to make a life there.

The samurai were a warrior class of nobility in Japan. Although Matsu is a servant, usually thought of as a lower social position, he proves himself to be noble and admirable, like a samurai.

Michiko

Michiko was the old woman who took care of Sachi when she first came to Yamaguchi. She appears in the novel only in Sachi's stories of the past. Michiko was so disfigured by leprosy that at first Sachi was afraid of her, but then Sachi was able to look past her appearance and came to see her wisdom and kind heart. Sachi believes that Matsu and Michiko saved her from her thoughts of suicide when she first contracted leprosy.

Pie

See Penelope Chan

Sachi

Sachi was a beautiful young woman who was engaged to be married when leprosy struck her. From that point on, she lived on the outskirts of an isolated village. Her fiancé could not stand by her, and her family would have preferred for her to commit suicide rather than have to live with the shame she is made to feel about her illness. Matsu helped her build a life for herself, including a lovely rock garden where she found some peace and happiness.

Her strength and her deep relationship with Matsu are inspiring to Stephen, but he also helps her. Before Stephen came, Sachi had never left Yamaguchi, but when he is injured in a storm, her concern for him brings her back into Tarumi. She continues to visit the beach house and comes to Kenzo's funeral, although he had hurt her and said hateful things to her. Her leaving Yamaguchi is important because it shows that she is opening her heart a bit more to the world after hiding away for almost forty years. By the end of the novel, she tells Stephen that he has become like a son to her and Matsu.

Tomoko

Tomoko is Matsu's younger sister. She died many years before the story takes place. She was very close friends with Sachi. Tomoko was one of the first people in Tarumi to show symptoms of leprosy. She killed herself because she felt that the disease had dishonored her family. Her death brought Matsu and Sachi together. Matsu brought Sachi Tomoko's lucky rock after her death, so when Sachi first suspected she herself had leprosy, she felt she could trust him.

Yoshiko

Yoshiko is Mr. Chan's mistress. She does not appear in the story, but she has an impact on Stephen's relationship with his father. After Stephen learns of the affair, he cannot see his father in the same way. Stephen's discovery of his father's infidelity is a loss of innocence for him.

Themes

Isolation

Throughout *The Samurai's Garden*, there are ways that the characters are isolated. Perhaps the most obvious example is Stephen. At the start of the novel, he must leave his home and travel to Japan to recover from an illness. He feels lonely in Tarumi, where he is both physically isolated from his family and socially out of place: he is an outsider, a young Chinese man in a Japanese town where many of the young men have gone to join the army.

There are also examples of the divisions of social classes that isolate people from one another. Stephen's father admits that when he was young, he thought that Matsu's sister was pretty, but they were "kept apart by class and custom." The distinction between employer and servant is a blurry line. Both Matsu and Ching have worked for the Chan family so long that they are like members of the family, but there is a certain reserve and respect that the servants must always maintain for their masters. For example, Stephen remembers Ching waiting for Mr. Chan "to taste the food and give his approval." She "appeared as anxious as a small child." Stephen describes how he "always felt uncomfortable being waited on." He does not like to be reminded of the differences in their social positions.

The village of Yamaguchi is also an important

symbol of isolation in the novel. The people there have been cast out by their families and their communities and forced to live apart from the rest of the world. Many people afflicted with leprosy feel so rejected and isolated because of their disease that they, like Matsu's sister Tomoko, commit suicide. Tsukiyama does, however, offer a hopeful note: the people living in Yamaguchi have banded together to create their own strong community, helping each other in bad times and celebrating the happy times.

Family Relationships

In *The Samurai's Garden*, Tsukiyama explores different types of family relationships. At first, Stephen's family does not seem to be at all close. When Stephen remembers a summer at the beach house in Tarumi years before, it certainly does not sound like the ideal family vacation: "My father had remained in Kobe that time because of business, while my mother spent most of each day alone in the garden, shaded from the sun by a large, red-paper parasol." We also learn that the children do not live at home: Stephen is in school in Canton, while Anne and Henry are studying in Macao. The family situation seems even more hopeless when Stephen learns that his father has been having an affair for twelve years.

However, Stephen and Pie are close, and in spite of Mr. Chan's mistress, Stephen's parents seem to want to try to stay married. Stephen's relationship with his father is strained, but in some ways they know each other better by the end of the story than they did at the beginning. Stephen might not approve of his father's affair, but it helps him understand why his father has always divided his time between Hong Kong and Kobe. For the first time, Mr. Chan shows some slight interest in Stephen's painting rather than dismissing it as unimportant.

Perhaps the strongest, most positive model for the importance of family in the novel is Matsu. Although when Matsu is first introduced, Stephen writes that "Matsu has lived alone … for the past thirty years," the reader gradually discovers that Matsu is far from alone. He has an extended network of family and friends. He and his sister Fumiko still seem close, although she no longer lives in Tarumi; he often sees his friend Kenzo; and he has extended his affection and protection throughout the entire village of Yamaguchi.

Topics for Further Study

- Rather than a garden with lots of plants and trees, Matsu creates a rock garden for Sachi. She uses a rake to trace patterns in the pebbles. With print and online sources, research Japanese rock gardens and how they relate to Zen Buddhism. Find images of gardens that you find beautiful and, using a program like PowerPoint, create a presentation to demonstrate the importance and beauty of these gardens to your class.

- Although the main story in *The Samurai's Garden* takes place in a peaceful seaside town, the war in China is often a worry in the back of Stephen's mind as the Japanese army makes its way closer to his home in Hong Kong. Research Japan's attacks on China in 1937 and 1938. Make a time line that compares historical events with the events of the novel. Note the differences in what Stephen hears on the radio in Japan versus what he learns in letters from his friend King.

- In *Why Does the Coquí Sing?*, by Barbara Garland Polikoff, teenager Luz Sorrento moves from Chicago to Puerto Rico. Just as Stephen feels out of place when he first comes to Tarumi, sure that he will be bored and lonely, Luz is certain that she will not like living in Puerto Rico, but both Stephen and Luz find a place in their new homes. Read *Why Does the Coquí Sing?* and write an essay comparing Luz's coming-of-age journey with Stephen's, noting what people and events help them along the way.

- *The Samurai's Garden* is made up of Stephen's journal entries during his time in Tarumi. Think about the story from the other characters' points of view. For example, what does Kenzo feel when he comes to Matsu's garden and finds Sachi there? What goes through Matsu's mind when he learns that his friend Kenzo has committed suicide? Why does Keiko tell Stephen that she cannot see him any longer? Choose an important scene in the novel and write a journal entry as if you are that character, describing in detail what happened and how you would feel in that situation.

It seems that Tsukiyama does not believe that one's family must include only blood relatives.

There are several examples of people being cared for by someone other than their parents. Michiko adopts Sachi when she comes to Yamaguchi, afraid. Matsu takes Stephen under his wing, and it seems impossible to disagree with the fact that Sachi and Matsu have become a family, although they are not related and are never married in the legal sense. Sachi welcomes Stephen into their family, as she explains to him near the end of the novel: he has become like their child, giving them "the one thing we've lacked."

Style

Symbolism

The title of *The Samurai's Garden* is an important cue to the reader: gardens are a central symbol in the story, and by examining the role the gardens play, the reader can understand more about the characters. Throughout the novel, comparisons and connections Tsukiyama makes between the characters and the garden or the earth symbolize something that is grounded, restorative, and good. Sometimes the references are fleeting, as when kind and patient Michiko is described as being "as silent as the earth." In other places, the relationship is more extensive, such as Stephen's interaction with Matsu's garden at the beach house.

At first, Stephen sees the garden's "quiet beauty," but his first response is to try to capture that beauty in a painting. Stephen calls the garden "seductive," and it is, but not in a negative sense: the garden draws Stephen out into life instead of letting him hide himself away. In several places, Tsukiyama shows how tending the garden leads to healing. For example, after Stephen is injured in the big storm, he and Sachi work to help Matsu repair the damage in the garden. Stephen writes in his journal, "Each day I work in the garden with Sachi, I feel stronger. The headaches lose their urgency once my hands dig deep into the cool, dark soil and

I smell the damp dirt and pine."

Sachi's garden also helped her to heal. She explains to Stephen how she rebuilt her life with Matsu's help: "As if I were a child learning to walk again, Matsu enticed me to take one step at a time: Bringing me first to Yamaguchi, then building me a house, and finally, creating this garden for me to tend." Sachi does not want flowers and plants in her garden. The fact that her garden is made of rocks and pebbles echoes the fact that her life may not be quite as full and rich as it would have been without her disease and isolation, but still the rocks are from the earth, and the garden helps her heal.

Epistolary Novel

An epistolary novel is one written as a series of documents. Often epistolary novels are in the form of letters, but they can also include diary entries, as in *The Samurai's Garden*; newspaper articles; and other documents. Because *The Samurai's Garden* consists almost completely of Stephen's journal entries, the reader gains an in-depth perspective on his thoughts, feelings, and motivations. Tsukiyama includes a few letters, which, along with the dialogue and some flashback stories that Stephen transcribes in his diary, provide hints of what other characters are thinking. When the story is largely limited to only one character's thoughts and feelings and told in the first person (where the narrator refers to himself as "I"), however, the reader must be careful not to assume that the words are unbiased truth. The story is not told by an impartial narrator, so everything has the slant of Stephen's own prejudices and possible misunderstanding.

Historical Context

Sino-Japanese War

In the mid-nineteenth century, Japan was an isolated country. Its leaders refused to allow trade with other nations, and for the most part, people maintained their traditional culture and way of life. Things began to change in July of 1853, when Commodore Matthew Perry of the US Navy demanded that Japan open its ports to trade with the West. Almost a year of negotiations followed, with Commodore Perry returning to Japan several times, but at last, on March 31, 1854, the Japanese signed the Treaty of Kanagawa, in which they promised to provide provisions for American ships and help shipwrecked American sailors. When the treaty was signed, Japan still did not want to allow trade but eventually gave in on this matter as well. The country underwent a rapid change from a largely agricultural economy to a modern industrialized nation. Japan is a relatively small island nation, however, and began to look to its neighbor, China, when it required more resources and a bigger economic market.

China was also a country that maintained its traditional society and politics. It was ruled by emperors until 1911, when revolutionaries proclaimed the first Chinese republic. Sun Yat-sen was elected president, but the new republic was not strong. It lacked military force, and for a decade, warlords squabbled over control of Beijing, the capital city. A group called the Guomindang became powerful, and a man named Chiang Kai-shek became their leader.

With the help of the Soviet Union and the Chinese Communist Party, which was also gaining in strength at the time, Chiang and the Guomindang managed to take control of China from the warlords. Then the Guomindang turned their attention to reducing the power and influence of the Communists. Some things improved under the republican government, but the day-today lives of most Chinese citizens did not change, so people increasingly looked to the Communists to make substantial changes.

In addition to the political turmoil inside China, diplomatic relations with Japan were worsening. In 1931, Japan attacked Manchuria, in the northeastern part of China, beginning years of armed conflict between the two countries. The League of Nations condemned the attack, but Japan refused to yield. Chiang chose not to confront Japan, however, and instead continued to direct his military power against the Communists.

The Japanese marched through China, taking control of much of the coast and many of the major cities. The Japanese army was notoriously brutal, killing and torturing civilians. Looting and arson were also common. The Chinese government estimates that as many as three hundred thousand people were killed in the Nanjing Massacre in 1937.

Japan disputes this figure, claiming that number to be closer to forty thousand. Japan's attacks on China and the acts committed by the Japanese military have created a lasting rift between Japan and China that still sours relations between the two countries. Japan's aggression also angered more established Western world powers, contributing to the global conflicts that sparked World War II.

Critical Overview

Reviews of *The Samurai's Garden* vary widely. All of the reviewers claim to find the story interesting, but several complain of Tsukiyama's writing style. Writing for *Library Journal*, for example, one reviewer says the novel has "the potential to be a winner" but "is sunk by a flat, dull prose style, one-dimensional characters who fail to engage the reader's interest, and the author's tendency to tell rather than show." Similarly, the writer for *Kirkus Reviews* describes the story as "slow and detached" and criticizes Stephen's journal entries as "lacking emotion and passion." Even his romance with Keiko "does nothing to bring out his oblique personality." The reviewer concludes that *The Samurai's Garden* is an "engaging story … dulled by the dim voice of its narrator" and seems to include both Tsukiyama and her character Stephen in this critique.

The Samurai's Garden is not the only one of Tsukiyama's novels to receive such harsh reviews. Her next novel, *The Street of a Thousand Blossoms*, is also criticized for its style. This novel is about two brothers, one who wants to become a sumo wrestler and one who hopes to make masks in a traditional Japanese Noh theater. Louisa Thomas, in a *New York Times* review, says that Tsukiyama's prose is simple and slow, at times seeming to strive for the kind of eloquence found in a Noh play, whose centuries-old art depends on stylized action to create tension and drama…. But the evident care that Tsukiyama takes in her language is sometimes undermined by the hard task of communicating a wealth of technical and historical information. It is also weakened by trite phrasing.

Compare & Contrast

- **1937–1938:** Japan attacks China in the hope of gaining control of the vast country, its economy, and its resources.

  Today: There is still political tension between China and Japan. In the summer of 2012, a dispute between the two countries regarding a chain of uninhabited islands (which provide access to huge deposits of oil and natural gas) in the East China Sea flares up. The conflict is believed to be fueled by Japan's past treatment of China.

- **1937–1938:** The Japanese army is merciless, killing not just Chinese soldiers but also civilians. Japan also uses germ warfare and brings some Chinese citizens back to Japan as forced labor.

  Today: Many Chinese citizens are still furious about Japan's actions in the war. In Beijing, there is a Museum of the War of Resistance against Japanese Aggression, and in 2005 the London *Independent* quoted a young schoolteacher visiting the museum: "I feel angry about the Japanese and their extremely cruel behavior towards the Chinese people." Some survivors of mistreatment continue to fight for compensation from the Japanese government.

- **1937–1938:** When left untreated, leprosy causes sores on the skin, muscle weakness, and nerve damage. Doctors understand that the disease does not spread easily, but many people fear catching leprosy and force those afflicted to less-populated areas. The available treatments are fairly ineffective.

  Today: Leprosy is sometimes called Hansen's disease. Modern antibiotics can kill the bacteria that cause the illness, and those with the disease are no longer isolated in "leper colonies."

Other reviewers disagree, approving of Tsukiyama's style. A review in *Publisher's Weekly* describes the novel as "beautifully crafted" and asserts that "Tsukiyama's writing is crystalline and delicate, notably in her evocation of time and place." Donna Seaman in *Booklist* agrees, calling

The Samurai's Garden "an extraordinarily graceful and moving novel about goodness and beauty" and naming Tsukiyama "a wise and spellbinding storyteller."

In *A to Z of American Women Writers*, Kort also calls Tsukiyama a "gifted storyteller." Kort believes that Tsukiyama's writing is "controlled and straightforward but also richly descriptive" and praises in particular Tsukiyama's ability to portray "the challenging lives of Asian women realistically but with dignity and sensitivity."

What Do I Read Next?

- In *Women of the Silk* (1991), Tsukiyama brings to life the world of silk workers in a Chinese village in the 1920s. The young women become friends and go on strike to improve their working conditions.

- Looking for his place in the world, a Mexican American teenager struggles with his family and neighborhood gangs in *Parrot in the Oven: Mi Vida* (2004) by Victor Martinez. This coming-of-age novel is a string of vignettes rather than a single continuous narrative.

- The Sino-Japanese War does not often receive much attention in itself because it contributed to the start of the larger conflict of World War II. *When Tigers Fight: The Story of the Sino-Japanese War, 1937–1945* (1983), by Dick Wilson, is one of the few histories of the war written in English. Wilson uses firsthand accounts to bring the events of the war to life.

- Amy Tan's *The Joy Luck Club* (1989) tells the story of four Chinese American women and their daughters. Jing-Mei, one of the younger generation, learns that her mother abandoned twin babies while fleeing a Japanese attack during World War II. Like *The Samurai's Garden, The Joy Luck Club* explores themes of cultural identity and portrays strained relationships between parents and children.

- *Snow Country* (1956), by Nobel

Prize–winning author Yasunari Kawabata, is considered a classic of Japanese literature. Set in a hot-spring resort in Japan's coldest region, the novel portrays the melancholy love affair between Shimamura, a wealthy, self-centered gentleman from Tokyo, and Komako, a local girl struggling to become a successful geisha.

- *The Good Earth* (1931), by Pearl S. Buck, tells of life in a rural Chinese village. It was influential in creating public sympathy for China and animosity toward Japan on the eve of World War II.

Sources

Andressen, Curtis, "Japan–Profile," in *Encyclopedia of Modern Asia*, Vol. 3, edited by Karen Christensen and David Levinson, Charles Scribner's Sons, 2002, pp. 204–10.

"Conversations: Acclaimed Novelist Gail Tsukiyama," in *Water Bridge Review*, http://www.waterbridgereview.org/122007/cnv_tsuk (accessed August 30, 2012).

Eimer, David, "Chinese Look Back in Anger at Japan's Wartime Atrocities," in *Independent*, August 15, 2005, http://www.ezilon.com/information/printer_7957.sht (accessed September 13, 2012).

"Gail Tsukiyama's Biography" Red Room website, http://redroom.com/member/gail-tsukiyama/bio (accessed August 30, 2012).

Kenley, David L., "Republican China," in *Encyclopedia of Modern Asia*, edited by Karen Christensen and David Levinson, Vol. 5, Charles Scribner's Sons, 2002, pp. 78–80.

Kich, Martin, "Tsukiyama, Gail," in *Encyclopedia of Asian-American Literature*, edited by Seiwoong Oh, Facts on File, 2007, p. 291.

Kort, Carol, "Tsukiyama, Gail," in *A to Z of American Women Writers*, Facts on File, 2007.

"Leprosy: Hansen's Disease," National Center for

Biotechnology Information website, http://www.ncbi.nlm.nih.gov/pubmedhealth/PMH00 (accessed September, 2, 2012).

Meyers, Chris, "Japan Nationalists Land on Isle at Heart of Row with China," in *Reuters*, http://www.reuters.com/article/2012/08/19/japan-china-idUSL4E8JH37C20120819 (accessed September, 2, 2012).

"Nanjing Massacre," in *Encyclopedia of Modern China*, edited by David Pong, Vol. 3, Charles Scribner's Sons, 2009, p. 282.

Review of *The Samurai's Garden*, in *Kirkus Reviews*, January 1, 1995, https://www.kirkusreviews.com/book-reviews/gail-tsukiyama/the-samurais-garden/#review (accessed September 3, 2012).

Review of *The Samurai's Garden*, in *Library Journal*, Vol. 120, No. 3, February 1995, p. 184.

Review of *The Samurai's Garden*, in *Publishers Weekly*, Vol. 242, No. 5, January 30, 2005, p. 85.

Seaman, Donna, Review of *The Samurai's Garden*, in *Booklist*, Vol. 91, No. 13, March 1, 2005, p. 1180.

Thomas, Louisa, "Orphans of War," in *New York Times*, October 14, 2007, http://www.nytimes.com/2007/10/14/books/review/1 t.html (accessed September 3, 2012).

Tsukiyama, Gail, *The Samurai's Garden*, St. Martin's Griffin, 1994.

Further Reading

Mehta, Geeta K., Kimie Tada, and Noboru Murata, *Japanese Gardens: Tranquility, Simplicity, Harmony*, Tuttle Publishing, 2008.

> The text and striking photographs in this book illustrate the techniques and elements that make Japanese gardens unique.

Tsukiyama, Gail, *The Street of a Thousand Blossoms*, St. Martin's Press, 2007.

> Tsukiyama is fascinated by specialized communities, for example the town of Yamaguchi in *The Samurai's Garden*. This interest is reflected in her novel *The Street of a Thousand Blossoms*. Tsukiyama writes of two orphaned brothers, each of whom looks forward to a career in Japanese tradition. Kenji hopes to make masks for Noh theater productions, and his older brother, Hiroshi, wants to be a sumo wrestler.

Yamamoto, Tsunetomo, *Bushido: The Way of the Samurai*, edited by Justin F. Stone, translated by Minoru Tanaka, Square One Publishers, 2001.

> Yamamoto was a samurai of the late seventeenth and early eighteenth centuries. This book translates his

writings, which describe the principles of the samurai class, including the central traditions of service and loyalty.

Yang, Gene Luen, *American Born Chinese*, Square Fish, 2008.

In this graphic novel, which is popular with young-adult readers, Yang introduces Jin Wang, a Chinese American student who longs to fit in. Using humor and fantasy, the book tackles issues of cultural stereotypes and identity.

Suggested Search Terms

Gail Tsukiyama

Gail Tsukiyama AND heritage

Gail Tsukiyama AND social groups

The Samurai's Garden

Japanese rock gardens

Sino-Japanese War

seppuku

leprosy

CPSIA information can be obtained
at www.ICGtesting.com
Printed in the USA
LVHW080912120822
725729LV00009BA/402